Sensitive, easy to read, and easy to understand. The examples you used touch a chord and treat children as people, not as inventory to be labeled, categorized, and organized by dysfunction. The Source helps you understand students' behavior by offering refreshing insights into their thoughts and feelings. The Resource challenges teachers to go beyond what's offered by "how to" books.

Herbert G.W. Bischoff, PhD, Former President
International School Psychology Association

This book should be on every teacher's desk. The short, stimulating passages allow it to be used as a creative resource on those impossible and time-precious days. Responding creatively and positively to troubled students at difficult times is one of the most challenging aspects of our profession.

Lois Jaeckel, Special Education teacher (EB/D)

It made me laugh, it made me cry . . . I'll always have a copy in my classroom.

Deb McKeon, SED Educator

I think this book is one of the most wonderful pieces I have read in years. I think it should be required reading for people working with all kids, not just 'special kids.' I have used the material in workshops and it has been well-received everywhere.

Sandy Queen, Director of Lifeworks

I really enjoyed reading your book. Even though I've worked with troubled kids for many years, I need reminders of some of their thoughts and feelings just to keep me on the right track.

Susan Bettinger, SED educator

This book—with its crisp, straightforward, and child-affirming advice—will be a lifesaver.

NAPRA Trade Journal

What Do You Do with a Child Like This? provides a thoughtful and penetrating view of troubled children—from the outside looking in and, perhaps more importantly from the inside looking out. It provides practical suggestions and inspirational messages to adults who work with troubled youth.

Randy Sprick, PhD, author
The Solution Book and *Discipline in the Secondary Classroom*

WHAT DO YOU DO WITH A CHILD LIKE THIS?

Inside the Lives of Troubled Children

L. Tobin

A notebook of thoughts, anecdotes and specialized techniques for teachers, counselors, psychologists, day care workers, and parents who find themselves in the adventure of working with children, especially troubled children.

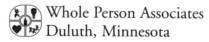
Whole Person Associates
Duluth, Minnesota

What Do You Do With a Child Like This?
Inside the Lives of Troubled Children

Whole Person Associates
210 West Michigan
Duluth, MN 55802-1908
(218) 727-0500
e-mail: books@wholeperson.com
http://www.wholeperson.com

Printed in the United States of America

10 9

BK
$19.95

Editorial Director: Susan Gustafson
Manuscript Editor: Kathy DeArmond
Art Director: Joy Morgan Dey
Production Coordinator: Paul Hapy

Library of Congress Cataloging in Publication number: 91-65948

ISBN 0-938586-44-0

The Source
A journey inside the lives of troubled children

The flow of topics through *The Source*

The Source teaches you to be—through your intuitive understanding of the child's inner needs—the best source of creative ideas for working with your child.

The Resources
The tools to create change in troubled lives

Introduction

You may teach successfully for years and never encounter a truly troubled child.

But sooner or later, a special child will walk through your door and you will find yourself saying, "What do I do with a child like this?" This child may not respond to rewards, and may seem indifferent to consequences; he may even reject your compliments and seem intent on making enemies rather than friends. Confused, you will recognize that all of the techniques that you've used effectively for years fail to reach through to this particular child.

How to begin?

You must dare to start over. You must search through your lifetime of knowledge, memories, and understanding to stimulate the creation of a whole new *bag of tricks* for reaching this child. You will pull new ideas from this bag of tricks until you find the key to this child, for this moment—and receive a richly rewarding glimpse of the joyful child within.

Then you must be willing to see your approach fail, and to begin your search all over again. Therein lies the adventure of working with troubled children.

What Do You Do With a Child Like This is a selection—in two parts—of insights and specialized techniques proven effective in working with troubled children.

The Source will take you on a journey inside the troubled child's world. You will discover that you can be (and are!) the best source of ideas for understanding and meeting the needs of your particular child.

The Resources will give you a diverse selection of methods and techniques for dealing with difficult behavior. You will find each of these techniques to be more creative and effective with troubled children than simple rewards or the pursuit of yet another consequence.

This book will take you inside the sometimes-troubled life of a child, and enable the two of you to walk out . . . together.

To be effective, you must dare to start over—to search for a whole new set of tools to reach through the facade of misbehavior to the troubled child hiding within.

The Source

A journey inside the lives

of troubled children

The challenge

TEACHING a troubled child is the consummate teaching experience, the ultimate challenge to your abilities, the perfection of the teaching art. It would seem unfortunate to teach for twenty years and never have a truly troubled child in your class to test your abilities.

Of course, no one ever said it would be easy—but perhaps no one ever told you it could be this rewarding either.

Seated in the back of the class, I remove myself from this world. I pile my books high on the front of my desk. I am a fortress, strong and impenetrable. No one sees me. Now I no longer wonder why no one reaches out to me. Look at me, I am a fortress, untouchable. Not even you, Teacher, ask me to take down my fortress walls—though often I wish someone would.

—Kevin

TO BEGIN, observe—but on the intuitive level. No checklists, no notes, no histories—just watch him. Watch him watching the world. Match his breathing. Go silently behind his eyes to see *his* world. When you *see* what he *feels*, you will have learned all that you need to know. Then begin.

WATCH LITTLE CINDY when the teacher loudly scolds her for pushing another first-grader. Is it a look of total indifference? total defiance? or is it something else? Watch her eyes closely. She's not there, simply not present. She's shut down, unable to handle the intensity of emotion.

If you heard the incessant screaming she suffers in her home, then you'd understand how useful that ability has been to her.

Just direct her to another activity; discuss the incident later. When engulfed in an adult's emotions, she goes elsewhere—to a safer place—within.

THE MISBEHAVIOR of troubled children is seldom what it first appears to be. Understanding this, I believe, is the only place to start. No child has a need to create a life of conflict.

Think about it—what need is the child trying to express?

CHILDREN whom teachers have learned to dislike are the most challenging. Skylar, age six, intimidates adults. See her now with the principal, laughing at him as he scolds her. Or is she?

If the principal looks closely, he will recognize her laughter to be an anxious scream, a mask for the terror she feels. But what strength it takes for him to see through her bizarre laughter to the scared little girl beneath!

Never has a child needed a hug more, and never has an adult been less inclined to offer it.

But he will hug her and the shell will begin to crack.

IF YOU are drawn to education, and if you enjoy a challenge, there is no greater challenge than to walk alongside a troubled child and to help her see a better world.

Inner needs   HE'S VIOLENT, you say.

Perhaps. But imagine what it takes for a child to strike an adult—his only source of survival. Imagine the depth of terror behind this bravado—like a parachutist slashing at the very ropes that protect him. Imagine the depth of hurt.

Each day you make me come to this school. No one likes me here. It's been this way since first grade. So I fight. At least then they notice me—they can't look through me when I hit them. At least then I don't feel invisible. I don't know for sure if there is more to school than learning to fight, but I know that there can be less.

—Neal

Imagine the depth of hurt. . . .

I'VE NEVER KNOWN a child to isolate himself by choice—
never—maybe because of a lack of opportunities or a lack
of skills. But never out of true choice—never!

APRIL, a kindergartner, grew up alone. When she entered
school, she was simply fascinated with other children. To
get their attention, she grabbed kids around their necks at
recess, all the while smiling. When she clutched at them
kids called her "the mean girl," and at first we agreed. They
screamed and she was punished. No one was getting
anywhere.

Finally we changed our approach. "April, are you trying to
play with that girl?" we asked. "Here's how you touch
when you want to play," we said. We then asked another
child to show April how. When she was no longer seen as
mean, other kids rallied to her—helping her learn to play.
We all just needed to understand differently.

I'VE YET TO MEET a troubled child who wasn't, above all else, terribly lonely. I presume loneliness even before I see the child.

It is six months into the school year. Yet each day you watch me play alone at recess. I play beside kids, but I play alone. No one picks me. They ignore me when I approach. You feel sorry for me, I know. But you are the teacher—the Creator of Games. They listen to you; they obey you. Can't you make it a game to figure out how to include me? You are the only person strong enough to make them stop to see who I am. . . .

—Craig

A CHILD will do almost anything to maintain his role in the group, whether he chose that role or was thrown into it.

What is the child's desired role? More importantly, does he have the skills to change that role if he so chooses?

I HATE TO SEE THIS. He's a good teacher; but ordering this six-year-old to sit down, then standing over her until she does, is a battle he will surely lose.

Abused since age three, her ability to stand up to adults is the only thing that has kept her alive. If he tells her to be seated and then steps away, she'll sit down shortly. I guarantee it. But this girl is strong and determined when confronted. That's what adults taught her to be.

EMOTIONALLY disturbed kids are distinguished by their regrettable ability to elicit from others exactly the opposite of what they really need.

THERE IS SOMETHING to be admired about children who can stand up to you and tell you what they think of you. It is a raw courage that, when channeled and nurtured, will serve them well. They will do all right in life, eventually. I don't worry about them.

NOW about those *regular* kids who do only what they are told and are afraid to tell you what they think about you, they're the ones I worry about. What about them?

I'm the only child of busy, successful parents. I'm busy, too. I really don't have time for the foolish things my seven-year-old classmates do. You can understand that, Teacher. You see, I need to grow up as fast as possible, so I won't be a bother at home. You tell me to go outside and play, but I'd rather stay with you. Adults like it when I talk in big words. Let me stay with you. No one needs me to be a child.

—Kristi

SO MANY troubled children keep jackets or caps on during the day. They need the physical protection for a fragile psyche; or perhaps they simply don't feel welcome and are keeping themselves ready to leave.

The jacket will come off when the child feels a sense of purpose and belonging.

YOU, CAROLYN, are an inspiration. In your five years you've been through more pain than most of us will experience in a lifetime. Yet you share with us each moment's joys; you smile and rush to the arms of every visitor to the class; and you tell them the wonders of your day.

Demanding? Well, yes, you are . . . demanding. But this is the first time in your short life that asking ever brought you anything.

And, yes, this world probably does owe you more attention than all the other students combined.

WHEN KELLY ARRIVED at the school she made cat sounds. She became known as the *cat girl*. Some kids thought it funny, at first; most thought it weird. Confused, we watched and conferred with each other. Weeks later a substitute teacher saw Kelly for the first time, heard the sounds and told her, "Stop that, it makes kids think you're weird." So she stopped.

EVERYTHING disturbed children do has a clear purpose to them and makes perfect sense within their view of the world. That's the fascinating puzzle—their view of the world.

Why do I steal? Why not? I'm not sure anybody cares what I do or what I want. So I take what I want. I want something that is a part of you . . . and you . . . and you . . .

—Annie

Dad left two years ago when I was seven. Mom stays at home; she wants to just spend her time with me and my younger sister. Mom talks to me like she used to talk to Dad. She's frustrated with her job. I'm not sure we'll make rent this month, and she still owes the plumber $234. We're worried about my sister's grades this week. I quit the baseball team and don't play with other kids very much so I can spend more time with her. She says she never misses Dad when I'm there. So I'll be Dad.

—Samuel

TROUBLED KIDS are more sensitive than other kids, although it may not seem that way. Most truly intuitive adults had this sensitivity as children.

Troubled children sense and feel beyond their ability to understand—though someday they will; someday this sensitivity will serve them well.

Behind troubled eyes

THERE IS SOMETHING about the eyes of abused children—a depth, a darkness, an absence of spirit. Scan any classroom and you will find those eyes. Scan any classroom and they will find you.

SEVERELY ABUSED CHILDREN show confused emotions. Their affect is off. They may laugh at scary moments or cry when surprised. They grew up ad-libbing parts in a play they never understood. For them nothing is natural. Direct them: "That man was hurt, this is not the time to laugh." Sadly, they must be taught the rules of natural response.

CHILDREN who have had everything taken from them as punishment—toys, food, friends—won't work for typical rewards. They've played that game with adults and always ended up losing. Only people-rewards will work—five minutes with the principal, lunch with the teacher, maybe time with the janitor. Moments of our time, our attention, are the only things they know we can never take back.

"ATTENTION SEEKING BEHAVIORS" is an unfortunate phrase. It sounds so devious. Children who *seek* attention are children who *need* attention. The behavior may be ignored, but not the need.

BEHIND EVERY ACT of misbehavior lies a strength—a desire to express needs and not give in. Children with less spirit give up, withdraw, or maybe just conform. You have to admire the vitality of spirit in children who are willing to fight.

JANICE pauses outside the classroom door, hesitating each time before she enters the room. She watches me, judging my mood. For her, watching people is more than a pastime: five minutes at home, and she may find her father in an uncontrolled rage. How helpless she must feel to have to watch her world so carefully—to fear changes in my mood that I hardly notice.

We struggled with this for weeks—until I learned to bring her in with a wink.

I sit in the back of the room, sleeve rolled up, and begin, slowly. This area on my arm is where it hurts best. Scratching, scratching, deeper. It feels good. You think it hurts, but you're wrong. Maybe it does hurt when the blood comes, but at least I know why it hurts; and when I want it to stop hurting, I stop. Is it so wrong to want one pain in my life that I understand?

—Marisa

EACH DAY the troubled child must balance the longing for security and consistency in life with the contradictory need to believe that life will be different tomorrow.

When the pain becomes great enough, a child will do almost anything to make tomorrow different than today.

SEVERAL mornings each month, Casey, 7 years old, trudges into class emotionally loaded. It hardly matters why. He sits quietly, beside my chair, at my side—sometimes for minutes, sometimes much longer—until he's ready to begin. We talk a lot. No schoolwork gets done this first hour, but it never did on these days, anyway. His body delivers the note that his mind will be arriving a little late this morning. We wait patiently together.

TEACH KIDS that they can affect their world. That is the most important thing of all.

Sharing the struggle

SOME KIDS, especially children of divorce, will insist on establishing a personal relationship with a teacher. They are tired of adults who direct their lives with minimal emotional involvement. "Are you willing to share who you are?" they wonder. "What are you doing in my life if you don't have time for a relationship with me?"

FOR THESE CHILDREN, especially, you must be as honest with your emotions as you ask your students to be with theirs—and that includes expressing frustration or anger when you feel it. Troubled children know when you are falsely pleasant and they recognize your hypocrisy. They need to see honest emotions and will push you until an honest emotion emerges. Control your anger and frustrations, but don't be afraid to show them.

I'M AWARE that at times I envy troubled kids—the intensity of emotion, the passion. I wish I could always be that passionate; I wish we all could emerge from behind our walls of propriety and convention. Sometimes I pause, chagrined. How misguided, how self-righteous it seems for me to discipline my troubled student for a depth of emotion I'm not sure I can even produce.

AT TIMES, so much of what I learned in education classes seems so irrelevant.

Huddled on the floor before me is a terrified ten-year-old—ten years of joys, discoveries, and fears, now in a state of total dysfunction. I hold her to keep her from falling apart. I know how to teach her math, and someday I will. But can I teach her to believe that her life will be better?

SOMETIMES I pause while a student plays out my own adolescent fantasies.

Steve and I both know that teacher was wrong to humiliate Steve's girlfriend in front of the class. I hold my comment for the moment. Steve, however, screams a protest right to the teacher's face.

Sometimes I envy the freedom of children to let the world know exactly how they feel. Sometimes it scares me.

HOW UNFAIR it seems that troubled children, who have such difficult, overwhelming lives, must bear the additional burden of knowing that they are seen as someone else's daily problem.

THE HURT that troubled children create is never greater than the hurt they feel.

WHEN I FIRST started working with troubled children, I was impressed by the effect of a few well chosen words— the power of a successful intervention. This feeling lasted for a time.

Then it began to scare me. "What if I say the wrong thing; make a mistake and damage a child?" I asked myself. That feeling also lasted for a time.

I know now that troubled children can no more be *destroyed* in a moment of error than they can be *cured* in a moment of glory. Still, sometimes I wish I hadn't learned that.

IN SOME PROFESSIONS, there are certainties—rules you can rely on, principles that hold true in every circumstance.

There are few certainties when working with troubled children. You try something, and if it fails you face the anger and frustration of a child who has already lived a life of failed efforts. The child's response to you is immediate and intense. You learn, maybe laugh, and go on. This ability to go on—to try again—may be the most important lesson you model to that child all year.

IF YOU CAN RISK an intuitive guess, dare to try anything and recover rapidly from mistakes, you will do well with troubled kids.

TEACHERS who are not experienced at working with troubled children tend to view difficult encounters with a child as a test of personal skills. They ask themselves, "Was I as skilled as I'm supposed to be? Did I resolve this problem. Did I do the right thing?"

Teachers who are experienced view difficult moments with a child simply as an opportunity to learn more about the child. They ask themselves, "Did the child respond to what I tried? What have I learned about what works and what doesn't work?"

I REALIZE that at times I am part of the problem—my personal reaction to the child keeps me from perceiving the child's true needs.

JAMIE, a bright, attractive, engaging 15-year-old, could have had the world at her feet. Instead she held back, unwilling to begin new assignments, unable to complete anything she started, all the while jumping from one abusive relationship to another. From some of the staff she evoked sympathy; from others, almost a perverse antipathy. She reminded each of us of the ultimately beautiful and talented person inside each of us, who, we too, often hid, denied, misused.

Jamie mirrored the saboteur within each of us. I watched myself react—at times caring, at times angry and often frustrated.

I seldom saw beyond the mirror to the discouraged girl who couldn't be cajoled into being what she didn't believe she was.

TROUBLED CHILDREN throw you back into the struggles of your own adolescence. Unresolved memories are rekindled.

Realize that you must resolve your own struggles before you can guide anyone else beyond theirs.

WORKING with rebellious kids, you will often walk the same tightrope they walk.

Carl, severely abused as a child, lives in opposition to authority—its rules and expectations. If I side with him—his need to aggressively assert himself, scream out his justifiable anger, and vent his distrust of adults—I'll run counter to rules and maybe to colleagues. If I don't validate Carl's frustrations, I will never be more than "just another teacher."

Today, Carl bolted out of history class rather than angrily confront his teacher. And they want to suspend him anyway.

I wonder what I'll say.

We walk this tightrope together.

TO RECOGNIZE and meet the needs of troubled children, you must recognize and meet the needs within yourself.

IF YOU WISH to hide from your own needs or escape from what is hurting within you, you can bury yourself in the drama of a troubled child.

You can devote your time to fixing a child's pain, and you may feel satisfied, for a while.

But soon the child's pain will become your pain; you will become overinvolved and lose perspective. Colleagues may applaud your devotion, but your methods will grow empty, limited by your own lack of awareness.

TROUBLED CHILDREN do not conceal their emotions well. They have a raw and disconcerting honesty. Perhaps that's why we call them difficult.

I HAVE LEARNED that the child who evokes my anger is a gift to me. He embodies the unresolved issues I carry at that time: rebellion, anger, selfishness, self-doubt—the hurt within me. As I work with this child I am invited to confront the passion of our shared struggle. I can respond or attempt to avoid it. But this child will force the issue—that is the gift.

Somehow, from somewhere, I must find the strength to overcome my struggle and to embrace this particular child . . . for he is the child within me.

I am the baby in my family. I shrug my shoulders and people take care of me. I never did anything for myself; I never had a chance to try. That was my role; now it's my act. I smile sweetly and watch you perform for me. And you will never see the anger I hold within me.

—Jessica

I DEVOTED so much time to Julie; she shared so much growth with me this year; now she is promoted to someone else's class. She had become a part of me, as much as my own child. Can I trust that teacher's skills? Will he understand her, and not let her fall back into old habits? How can I know for sure? How can I help but wonder if I don't hold back sometimes for fear of having to let go.

A REBELLIOUS CHILD seeks something in you with which to identify. I dress casually, sit on tables, or address teachers by their first names. As a counselor learns to parallel a client's speech and posture, I parallel a square life learning to function in a round hole. For me, and for most people in the counseling field, this comes quite naturally.

A TROUBLED CHILD needs most of all to spend time with adults who think life is worth living. He searches for reasons to struggle on to adulthood. Life must be seen as a worthwhile adventure before healing can begin.

THE RELIANCE on measurable behavior data has had the unfortunate effect of diminishing reliance on intuitive understanding. You must trust that you understand more about a child than you can prove that you know.

All teachers have the skills to work with troubled children. The needs of troubled children are not that different from the needs of the children you were trained to teach—just more immediate.

Creating change

IN THE FACE of misbehavior my job is to create a change in order to effect a change. I may change the structure of the classroom, the method of instruction, the peer interaction, my actions or thoughts or expectations, or I may simply command change in the actions of the child. Of these, the last is the least effective. "Shilo," I say, "I want you to pay attention now." Sound familiar?

WHEN YOU WANT something to change, you must change something.

BEHAVIOR MANAGEMENT must be more than just devising techniques to make children do what we want them to do.

We *can* do that; we have all the rewards and consequences and techniques. But do they meet the child's needs? Do they treat the child with dignity? A troubled child will answer these questions for you. You will know quickly and clearly whether you have met a need or only managed a behavior for a time.

THE GREATEST CHALLENGE is to recognize that the most offensive, belligerent child may only begin to respond to you after you initiate steps to reestablish the relationship. You must take the first step in a new direction.

STUDENTS WHO *cannot* or who believe they *cannot* become very skilled at making it appear that they *will not*.

Teaching styles

THERE ARE innumerable explanations for a child's behavior. Your explanation will dictate the intervention you select. If an intervention that *should* work does *not* work, take a second look at your assumptions.

It is valuable to make a brief note about each intervention you attempt. Alongside this note, record your assumption about the cause of the misbehavior. If the behavior is not improving, then every few days (or weeks) write a new assumption. Yes, a new assumption. New interventions will come to mind naturally.

YOUR ABILITY to accurately perceive a child's inner needs is the source for the most effective interventions available to you.

EVEN THE MOST experienced, successful teachers may have a difficult time when they first encounter a severely troubled child. It is difficult to accept that, with this child, they are back to square one. But that is the only way they can begin to understand.

SOME TEACHERS control their classrooms through their personalities by granting and withholding attention. Others exercise control through structure by establishing rules and contingencies. A troubled child requires both. Structure alone will control, but not heal the child; while the teacher who tries to manage a troubled child through personality alone will be eaten alive.

TEACHERS WHO DISCIPLINE through the force of their personal charm often have the most difficult time with severely troubled children. These teachers find it hard to accept that there are children who are disillusioned with all adults and who are indifferent to praise and disapproval. To these kids, it means nothing to receive attention or to have it abruptly withdrawn. That's all they've ever known. And they won't play that game anymore.

CONSISTENCY is the key component when working with troubled kids. But consistency is far more than just a rigid application of rules. What troubled children need consistently is to feel your openness and caring, your heart touching theirs. Sometimes this requires that you follow the letter of the rule; sometimes this means that you must bend it.

TEACHING physical wellness (exercise, nutrition, relaxation) is an essential, but often neglected, component in any program for troubled children. People of all ages must learn to manage stress effectively.

SOME student-teacher combinations are simply too volatile to be effective. Children raised by sarcastic parents may react vehemently to a sarcastic teacher, and only a change of placement can avoid a lost year.

Sometimes it is the only feasible, though uncomfortable, solution.

STAFF MEMBERS in every school possess a wealth of skills and ideas, and will share them if given the opportunity. The answer you seek may be just next door.

EACH YEAR'S CLASS has its own personality. Consider: if an individual child had the personality of this year's class, how would you adjust your teaching style to meet this child's unique needs? Each year your classroom management program must begin with just such an adjustment in your teaching style.

STAYING AFTER SCHOOL with the teacher can be a reward or a punishment. It all depends on the child and the circumstances. But nine out of ten times, in spite of what you think, in spite of the circumstances, it's a reward.

YET, ULTIMATELY, we teachers are the least important people in the classroom. We come and go—the students will spend the rest of their lives with each other. We are only visitors; they are family.

❖

Creative intervention

THE NATURAL INCLINATION is to attempt to control difficult children by suddenly making all classroom rewards contingent upon behavior. Everything they receive—recess, P.E., trips, Christmas parties—they have to prove they deserve. Was it ever like that when you were seven years old?

WHEN WORKING with discouraged children, I make two lists. One itemizes activities which they enjoy. I use this list for contingencies and rewards. The other shows what they value most in life, the things that make their day worthwhile. This list I *never* make contingent.

MANY TEACHERS who encounter a difficult child expect too much change too soon. List the behaviors you want to change. If you improved one behavior a week would it really take so long?

THE MORE SEVERE the consequence, the less likely it will be consistently applied. You'll hesitate, then wait until your level of frustration matches the severity of the consequence. Reasonable, consistent, incremental consequences help you avoid growing angry.

If removal from recess is an effective deterrent for a child, exclusion for one minute will probably be sufficient. Sixty seconds alone in the room is a long time. More importantly, you won't have used up all of your consequence material on one incident.

DISCIPLINE (read "punishment") is only a subset of a comprehensive behavior management strategy. It is what you resort to when a more creative approach escapes you. Reliance upon consequences asserts that the problem resides entirely within the child, not within the circumstances we have created. All too often, however, the circumstances in which we place the child do prompt the misbehavior.

CHILDREN capable of creative misbehavior will appreciate creative and innovative responses. It's an intellectual jousting match during which the child explores important themes such as power and authority and limitations. Nothing accelerates the contest more than the insult of a detached, systematic, mechanical response to explorative behavior.

YOU cannot be innovative if you fear the judgment of the unexpected observer. You must risk moments that could be misunderstood.

THE MOST DARING, even shocking, interventions are often the most effective. You must be willing to try; you must be willing to fail. Remember, people have tried the ordinary interventions with these kids for years, and have been unsuccessful.

AT ANY GIVEN MOMENT, any child would prefer to be seen by peers as *bad* rather than *dumb*. Some children make a career of it.

POSE QUESTIONS to the class, pause for thinking time, then select a student to answer the question. Eye contact alone will tell you who has the correct answer. In this way, you can increase the probability of correct responses from discouraged kids.

ALL CHILDREN reach an age when being given rewards—stickers, candy—becomes demeaning; when they realize they shouldn't need to be materially rewarded for everything they do. We recognize this as a sign of maturity, and so do they.

AFTER YOU ABANDON the search for the Magic Reward or the Magic Consequence, meeting the needs of children and teaching them to meet their own inner needs is what remains.

SOMEDAY I'll make a list of my great ideas that have failed: the reward party at the mall that resulted in two kids being expelled; prescribing the symptom of silence to an elective mute child, and getting more silence! The list of notable attempts goes on and on. If I ever begin to fear such attempts, I'll move on to other work.

WHEN A CHILD fails to earn rewards in a token reward system, it is simply not a reward system. I'm not sure what it is. Back to the drawing board.

SHAWANA AND I are pen pals. Each day she writes me a letter about her life—beautifully written expressions of the fears and joys of a thirteen-year-old. Each day I write back.

I am in constant awe of how openly she expresses herself in letters. You see, she doesn't speak to many adults. In fact, she's never spoken to me.

Don't say that I lie; that I didn't hit twenty home runs last summer, that I don't have a brother who plays for the major leagues. I don't tell lies, not real lies. Call them stories of my life. The life I wish I was living. That's no lie.

—Mario

SENDING A CHILD home in response to misbehavior delivers conflicting messages. It says to the child that he can express anger, but not too much; that he is accepted, but only on condition; that classroom learning is important, but he can be removed from it. A delinquent child may respond positively to suspension, but a troubled child will see this as another rejection. When you suspend a truly troubled child, you lose far more than you gain.

WITH SINCERE EFFORT and a broad repertoire of intervention strategies, you can expect to make changes in a troubled child's life, as long as changing the child is not your sole measure of personal success.

Classroom design

I USED TO PLACE difficult children in the front row of the classroom. This seemed to make sense. But watch someone teach from the front. Notice that most of the teacher's attention actually falls upon the second or third row and sweeps toward the middle of the back row. The front and back corners are blind spots where the least visual attention and fewest questions are focused. The child in the front row, below the teacher, is unable to watch instruction, avoids warning glances, and has the attention of everyone in the classroom. This is choice seating! In fact, I sat there through most of second grade, and loved it.

I FIND IT USEFUL to look at a room in terms of an energy system.

Carol's third grade students constantly fought among themselves. In tightly packed rows on one side of the room, they formed an energy block that Carol could not control from her desk across the room. Eventually she placed her desk in the center of the group. By inserting herself within the energy block, she became an active participant in the group's interactions and began to structure group cohesiveness.

TRAFFIC FLOW through a room is another part of the energy system. Where the energy flow is blocked, behavior problems will arise.

A TEACHER'S philosophy of education is evident in the structure of the seating.

Are the seats grouped together for cooperative learning and social skills development? Or is individual responsibility emphasized through placement in rows? More importantly, are the teacher's behavioral expectations consistent with the structure created?

SIMILARLY, teachers' perceptions of the teaching role are sometimes reflected by the placement of their own desk. I find front-desk teachers are more directive with students, consider themselves the focus of learning, and may tend toward authoritarianism. Side-desk teachers tend to guide students and are more inclined to encourage student interaction. Rear-desk teachers are more detached and objective. Or maybe that's just my imagination.

KIDS who have no space that they can call their own at home will go to great lengths to individualize and take ownership of a space at school. That space may be their only private place in their world.

A CHILD placed among a group of smarter students will improve his performance. Call it osmosis, call it peer influence if you like, but it's true. Unfortunately, this is not what we usually do with special children.

WE TAKE A CHILD with the least social skills, who cannot get along with anyone, and put him in a classroom with other children with similar inabilities to get along with anyone. Then we reward him when he manages to get along with the others. Somehow that just seems wrong.

INVARIABLY, the child placed in an isolated location in the classroom is the child who most needs social interaction. A brief time away—a few minutes or hours—will allow him to consider his actions, but he can only learn social behaviors when he returns to regular seating.

Isolated seating manages behavior, but doesn't help the child learn the specific interpersonal skills he lacks. And the cycle continues.

A CLASSROOM produces what it presents. A clean, organized classroom produces order. A messy, disorganized room, chaos. A stimulating, creative classroom is neither too clean nor too messy, but is filled with objects that produce thought and curiosity. What values does your classroom present?

Consider the posters, sayings, and pictures on your classroom walls. Are they sincere or cynical? What is the tone, the mood? What do the words *actually* say? Do the walls speak the messages that you want a child's subconscious to hear?

CLOSING MY EYES, I imagine myself seated in the student's chair. I become that student and ask myself: "Am I part of the group, or am I an outsider? Does the teacher have ready access to help or correct me, or am I just beyond reach? What's my view? What distracts me? What's within reach? How would I characterize those in my classroom neighborhood: movers and shakers? outcasts? shadows?"

What does the student's placement in the classroom communicate to him about his role in the classroom? I ask myself these questions to put into words what the student puts into self-expectations.

PROXIMITY CONTROL, being able easily to walk by trouble spots, is the highest priority in managing a difficult classroom.

No. A sense of humor is the highest priority!

STANDING in the doorway at the start of each class period provides an invaluable opportunity to acknowledge students as they enter, state your expectations for the first minutes of class, and intercept any behavior problems before they enter the classroom. The tone and mood are set before the bell rings.

THUMBNAIL ASSESSMENTS:

the kid with the messed up hair—learning disabled;
the kid with his jacket on all day—emotionally disturbed;
the kid with no friends—abused;
the kid in isolated seating—socially deprived.

Not totally accurate, but probably not far off.

Difficult lives

DURING the past thirty years the special education movement has uncovered many reasons why children have difficulty learning. It has taught us that the child who we previously thought failed to learn simply because he didn't want to learn did not exist.

WHEN I need to learn how a teacher perceives his ability to reach a troubled child, I ask him to fill out a behavior rating on that child. This rating is effective in helping me understand the teacher. Sometimes I also learn about the child.

CHILDREN who have Fetal Alcohol Effect (FAE) are not recent arrivals to the classroom. They are like the other troubled children we have been working with for years. Today, etiology is more clearly defined and there may now be a higher percentage of FAE children, but the problems are familiar. Same kids, different label.

Like all troubled children, FAE children will benefit from a classroom that resembles a well-run seminar: start on a positive note, present the schedule for the day, establish participant expectations, move smoothly into transitions, minimize outside distractions, provide plenty of social opportunities, and make learning an enjoyable experience so the children will want to return.

Whereas the LD (Learning Disabled) and SED (Seriously Emotionally Disturbed) children can escape their label, the FAE label is permanent. It is imperative to communicate to the child that the classification clarifies needs, but does not excuse misbehavior. Re-guiding the child's self-perceptions is perhaps the greatest challenge.

WHILE WE ARE understandably reluctant to identify young children as emotionally disturbed or behavior disordered, the early primary years remain the optimal times for effective intervention. Generally speaking, troubled children don't suddenly appear in the sixth grade. Red flags begin waving in kindergarten.

GIVE A TEACHER a reading method she believes in and children will learn to read. Give a student a teacher who enjoys life and the student will release his fears.

MOST CHILDREN who flit from one task to another do not have an attention deficit. They may simply need more stimulation, or they are lonely, or lost.

SAYING, "Sit on your fingertips," to a behaviorally disordered child may be the best way to quiet his body during instruction and to allow his mind to attend.

NOTES SENT HOME at the end of the day serve little purpose unless they are specific about what a good or bad day means.

AN ABUSED CHILD must gain confidence in his ability to stay in control of his world at all times. We must allow and encourage this additional degree of self-determination while he's at school. Rather than setting a deadline, I ask him, "When can I expect your assignment to be finished?" I urge him to participate in the decisions of his life.

ALLOW THE STUDENT to terminate any punishment with a statement of commitment: "Vaughn, stand by the wall until you can tell me you are ready to participate."

IGNORE MISBEHAVIOR at first. This will allow you to continue teaching, and will help you discover if the behavior was meant to attract negative attention.

YOU TELL ME that you hit your child at home so "he'll know better next time." But how will he know *differently* next time?

YOU CAN ONLY remove a behavior when you supply another behavior to replace it. "Don't . . . " is most effective when followed by "But you may . . . "

IT DEVASTATES some students to leave the classroom for remedial reading. We may not know why, what they've been told, what names they've been called. But until we do know, we need to find a way to bring special help to them rather than sending them elsewhere to seek it.

I'VE ALWAYS FELT that the tone I set during the first twenty minutes each morning influences the mood of troubled kids for the rest of the day. If I can convey sincere interest and reestablish behavioral expectations, the tone is set for a good day.

OFTEN WOMEN make the best teachers of emotionally disturbed adolescent boys. It reduces the male-male rebellion. Unless, of course, a boy has more issues with his mother.

IF I AM willing to take "no" for an answer, I ask the children, "How many think it's too noisy?" Although I sometimes lose with this approach, I always learn something worthwhile.

GOOD PRAISE, like good humor, depends mostly on timing and delivery.

I'VE NEVER HAD a serious argument with a child who accepted something to eat from me upon arriving at my office.

THE MOST POWERFUL rewards are not the earned rewards—they are expected. The most powerful rewards are the unexpected ones because they reward a child not for what he has done, but simply for who he is.

THINK ABOUT how much time a troubled child already takes up in your day—the total time you spend correcting and redirecting and disciplining him. Twenty-five minutes out of every morning, maybe more? If each day you scheduled five minutes of quality time with him, wouldn't the result be a net gain for everyone?

GIVE DISCOURAGED STUDENTS one task that makes them feel important. One clear reason for them to walk in the door.

Healing touch

ALL CHILDREN need to touch and be touched. You either structure it into the day, or you fight it all day long.

Teaching children about "bad touch" must be accompanied by teaching them how to give and receive "good touch": hugs, hand holding, massage, a pat on the back, a hand on the shoulder—the touch you also would enjoy.

The skin registers two qualities of touch. Light touch to our skin is stimulating; it alerts our senses. Deep touch—hugging, swaddling, massage, a hearty embrace—feels calming.

TO SETTLE an active child, hold him firmly by both shoulders. This physical directing can be calming, if the relationship and the moment are right. A hesitant or unsure touch is likely to agitate the child further.

IF YOU FEAR or dislike a child, your touch will immediately give you away. When you touch someone you communicate more clearly than with words.

I never touch a child when I am angry. Like most parents, I learned that the hard way.

They suspended me from first grade because I got mad and screamed and kicked the teacher. Why did she let me keep kicking her? Why didn't she stop me? It was scary to lose control of myself, but it was even more terrifying to see adults helpless to stop me.

—Ben

LIGHTLY TOUCHING or casually grabbing an agitated and angry child is asking for trouble. If the child is out of control and you must take physical control, take complete control.

Touch or take physical control of a child only when your intention is clear: when you know what you are going to do and why.

IF YOU FEEL helpless with a resistant young child, it may stem from your unwillingness to physically follow through on what you say—"You can walk back to your seat alone, or I can guide you." Follow through, but do it firmly, safely, and never in anger.

Troubled kids want to know if you have the commitment to follow through. If you are afraid to enter a child's physical space, you will never touch the child's world.

CHILDREN TIRE of adults who give directions without providing direction.

WE ALL CARRY tension somewhere in our bodies, but in some bodies the tension is more obvious than others. When Ed becomes agitated, his shoulders become tense and twitch. We taught him to be aware of this first body-signal that he was frustrated and beginning to lose control. Then we taught him how to relax, first his shoulders, then his mind. He is learning self-intervention, body-to-mind intervention. These are techniques he will value throughout his life.

SOME CHILDREN'S BODIES are not suited for sitting cross-legged on the floor. Although they are young, this posture is not physically comfortable for them. Asking these kids to sit on the floor is an invitation for them to misbehave.

As a seating option, consider providing narrow, rectangular beanbag cushions. Cushions straighten the spine when children sit cross-legged. They are also comfortable for children who prefer to sit back upon their heels. Children can select which style is most comfortable to them, reducing their restlessness.

ANOTHER INVITATION to misbehave is the requirement that children raise their hands to signal for the teacher's attention. This is physically exhausting for most children.

A child can continue to work while waiting for your attention if he places a book upright or raises a mailbox flag on the side of his desk.

Words, words, words

WHEN YOU COUNSEL troubled kids, their response to your words is less important than the seeds of thought you plant while talking with them. An angry mind is a mind that is open to suggestion. Pour in the positive statements—the affirmations of inner strength. Then step away. Thoughts need time to do their work.

WORDS trigger misbehavior as readily as actions. "You could have . . . " raises fewer defenses in their minds and is more instructive than "you should have."

IF I COULD permanently remove one phrase from my vocabulary it would be, "Why did you?" A child's answer is never satisfying. Kids don't know why. The question only frustrates both of us. I do better with "what" questions: "What was the problem that started the fight?" "What did you want?" "What do you need to let this go?" Through "what" questions you can teach "why" reasoning.

Another loaded phrase I avoid is "Why don't you?" as in, "Why don't you sit down now?" This is neither a question I want answered (e.g., "Because I don't want to.") nor is it a casual suggestion that a child is free to refuse. A simple command, "Please, sit down now," is clean and immediate. Listen to yourself talk, you can hear the difference.

"Would you like to get in line now?" I ask, knowing I can't take "no" for an answer. Most kids would step in line; troubled kids will answer my question. I can't help but smile—playing straight-man again to a too-quick fourth grader.

WHEN YOU'VE MADE a decision, state it and expect it to be carried out. Excess verbiage produces argumentative kids who may become great lawyers, but it doesn't help their behavior right now.

A QUICK OBSERVATION of a parent and child together reveals the verbal interactions that push the child's buttons. I record these and avoid them.

ON OCCASION I HEAR from teachers or parents, "I don't like you when. . . . " Could anyone possibly mean that? Criticize the behavior, never the child. "I don't like what you're doing," leaves the child intact.

IT IS SAFEST not to discuss the right or wrong of some things kids do: daydreaming or masturbating, for instance. Kids simply have to understand when these activities are appropriate and when they aren't.

The question of parenting

SOME CHILDREN simply fail to elicit nurturing. They have no idea how to reinforce a teacher or parent, and they are unaware of the benefits that come from complimenting or encouraging others. Fortunately this can be taught. It is an essential life skill.

SINGLE PARENT HOMES, distance from relatives, two working parents—parenting has never been lonelier than now. Many families are isolated and without support. Parents are not the problem; parenting is. There's a difference.

How can any teacher help but resent the additional responsibilities that once belonged to the home but now fall on the schools: sex-education, re-parenting, health, alcohol and drug education, personal safety. But schools teach what society feels children must learn. The responsibilities of teaching have changed, but the mission remains the same.

TEACHERS ARE OFTEN the only source of parenting suggestions for many young parents. I deeply regret conferences with confused parents in which I outlined school-based problems instead of subtly promoting home-based skills.

I CONSIDER IT good parenting when a child has one happy, vital parent. Two works even better. But all children need at least one vital parent to teach them about *happy*.

I'm like my Dad. He always acted up in school. He's told me all the stories about when he was a kid. He laughs about the things that I do. (Comparing stories are some of our most fun times). Mom doesn't like it much, but she's a girl and wouldn't understand about guy things. Dad hasn't come to a parent-teacher conference, but if he did he would explain about how much he enjoys the trouble I get into—at least I think so.

—Bobby

WITH TROUBLED CHILDREN I practice showing pleasure at what a child does well, curiosity and surprise at what a child does poorly. When I react as if I expect misbehavior, I can expect—misbehavior.

I DO NOT tell parents that teachers expect to be in control of their children. Parents are in control of their children; children are in control of themselves. Teachers, however, are in charge of the children. This wording is far less offensive, and probably more accurate.

STUDIES INDICATE that abusive parents often know how to praise and reward children just as well as non-abusive parents. However, abusive parents often lack the ability to selectively ignore minor misbehavior and to redirect the child toward a positive activity.

THAT CHILDREN always know how to entertain themselves in any situation is an adult myth that ignores the unfathomable boredom of many children's lives.

"You have germs," other kids said. That's how the first days of school began, but now they just ignore me. I know my clothes and hair are funny. You probably didn't want to, Teacher, but finally you spoke to my mother. She just didn't know how hard it is to be different. But you do, Teacher, and she listened. She didn't want me to be teased or different. She just didn't know."

—Joshua

THE POLICE are a part of the school's behavior management team, even in elementary schools and even in small towns. If a student's behavior is likely to put him in jail in later years, this is not only a school issue. He needs to learn that early.

Social services are also a valuable part of the school's behavior management team. Too often early signs of neglect and juvenile abuse are not reported. Later, when action against the family could protect the child from further abuse, the court system has no record of prior problems and cannot act. The school is a part of the community. Keep the community involved.

The counselor within

KYLE AND SACHA are fighting over the swing. They are learning how to communicate with each other. Who knows, they may be husband and wife some day and I may be their marriage counselor. What can I teach them at this moment about sharing and expressing needs that will save time for all three of us twenty years from now?

WHEN WE STEP IN just to stop an argument between kids, we prevent learning from taking place. If we lack the time to orchestrate a learning moment, it is better to walk away.

I BELIEVE there is a brief magical moment in every relationship when the right statement will change a life. On some level, everything we do with a child is preliminary to that one moment.

With each child . . . one moment.

IT IS DIFFICULT to avoid the word "should" when giving advice to a child who is working below his potential. I prefer to simply affirm to the child, "You will raise your grades when it becomes important to you." Then I say no more.

WE TEND TO VIEW misbehavior as resistance because we understand where we want children to go. Children view misbehavior as protection because they know where they've been.

THE MOST EFFECTIVE session with a child may consist of little more than one statement of reassurance, such as, "You'll be able to handle this." Forty- five minutes of talk can not achieve as much as one timely statement of trust.

WHEN I WATCH a confrontation between two children, I sometimes wonder how I would react if they were adults. How would I ask adults to solve the problem? Looking at it this way helps give a new perspective on what needs to be said. Adults or children, the needs are not that different.

Positive adult attention

TROUBLED CHILDREN expect you to be repulsed by the ugliness they see inside themselves. They expect you to choose to be with "better" kids. Somehow you must show them that you care deeply for the complex persons they actually are. You can do this out of unconditional love or simply because you know that we are all in this life together, struggling to make sense of it, each in our own unique way; and helping each other as opportunity allows.

HERE I AM, stuck in the classroom during lunch hour for the third day in a row. Once again, I find myself playing nursemaid to Ben with nothing to eat but my own hasty words of reprimand: "If you do that again, you'll stay in for lunch." I'm almost as amused as he is.

"Ben, let's take a walk outside and talk."

IF THERE IS A MAGIC REWARD, an optimal reinforcer, it is positive adult attention. Sometimes it is just that simple. The world has not changed that much since you and I were children.

The Resources

The tools to create change

in troubled lives

No book, no formula can provide you with a key to unlock the unique world of the troubled child in your life; but there are paths to guide you.

The Resources is a collection of these paths: a varied selection of techniques, perspectives, and conceptual tools to help put form to your thoughts about a troubled child.

As your work with troubled children begins with an understanding of their needs, *The Resources* begins with a conceptual framework to help you identify a child's unmet needs. In addition, *The Resources* gives you a quick-reading reference to a wide range of creative interventions to address misbehavior; provides new teachers with brief, thought-provoking introductions to numerous techniques that can be implemented without purchase of additional materials; presents adaptations of traditional approaches that may meet the unique needs of troubled children more effectively.

First-hour needs

Each of us begins the day hoping to meet our basic needs. Besides the obvious requirements—food, shelter, and security—we also strive for companionship, acknowledgment, humor, activity, and so forth. As adults, we understand that few of these needs must be met during the first hour of the day. We can wait to see friends until after work, eat later in the morning, feel the love of others throughout the day. Adults are able to delay their needs.

Troubled children, however, are unable to delay the fulfillment of basic needs. Lacking security in their lives, they struggle to meet essential needs as soon as possible. This struggle becomes a matter of survival to a degree most of us can hardly imagine. To a troubled child, nothing—certainly not math or reading—is more important than being reassured as early in the day as possible that he has food, friends, attention, and encouragement.

All students come to school with unmet needs. Most have the ability to delay these needs. Troubled children focus on nothing else until these needs are met. Meet the needs early or consume your time fighting them. The choice is yours, not theirs.

It is not difficult to determine a troubled child's primary unmet needs. An unmet need is made obvious by the child's inability (1) to *delay* meeting that need; (2) to *express* that need; or (3) to *elicit* a healthy response from others to that need.

If a child *cannot wait* to have a need satisfied, you will probably spend a lot of time fighting it: trying to keep the child from talking, touching, or eating.

If a child feels a need but is *unable* to express it, the absence of this natural response will become conspicuous. You may notice that he has no friends, doesn't like to play, or is afraid to laugh.

If a child *no longer believes* that others will fulfill his needs, you may be confused by the contradictory nature of what the child elicits from you and others. For example, unable to make friends, the child appears intent upon making enemies; or unable to experience structure and consistency in his life, he sets out to create hourly chaos.

Troubled children are distinguished most clearly by the frustrated expression of needs. They actively elicit the opposite of what they really need.

To identify a child's unmet needs, ask yourself: "what makes this child different? What does he spend his time doing or avoiding? What self-defeating response does he elicit that appears to be the opposite of what he really needs?"

Consider these common statements listed below. They describe responses to the unmet social need when (1) the child is unable to delay meeting it, (2) the child is unable to express the need, and (3) the child has given up.

(1) "He won't stop talking."

(2) "He doesn't seem to make friends."

(3) "He hurts kids and makes enemies."

The most essential step in any classroom behavior management program is to design the first hour of class to meet your troubled students' unmet needs.

On the following pages, the responses children make to their unmet needs are described. The list below summarizes these responses.

Summary of ten needs

the need	undelayable	unexpressed	frustrated
Acknowledgment	pester	withdraw	rebel
Nutrition	chew objects	tire easily	anger
Communication	annoy	appear distracted	act out
Socialization	talk incessantly	isolate	make enemies
Touch	touch excessively	provoke fighting	fear touch
Humor	clown around	be overly serious	be cynical or morose
Physical Activity	move restlessly	stretch	resist activity
Structure	demand consistency	resist change	create chaos
Relaxation	withdraw	agitate	appear oppositional
Encouragement	seek reassurance	avoid challenge	give up

I raise my hand each morning and tell you that I am "present," but no one ever talks to me. I walk to school alone. No one asks me how I feel, wishes me a good day at school, or even acknowledges that I am awake. Until someone stops long enough to look into my eyes, touch me, awaken my spirit, welcome me into the world, let me know that I matter—until then, how can I be sure that I am really "present?"

—Kayla

The need for acknowledgment

- The child who cannot wait for acknowledgment may pester for attention.

- If she cannot express the need for acknowledgment, she may appear lonely, lost in the crowd.

- If she no longer believes she can get acknowledgment, she may withdraw or rebel.

Being acknowledged by someone, welcomed into the world each morning, is as important to a child as a good breakfast. Acknowledgment "breaks the fast" of a lonely night, providing essential nutrients for the spirit.

Who could the child check in with each morning before class? A favorite teacher, principal, janitor?

What morning responsibility would give importance to his presence? What first-hour activity could put him in contact with at least one other student—get him involved?

I come to school hungry. Sometimes we have no food at home. Other times Mom wakes me up late and just pushes me out the door; I think that's when we don't have any food either . . . or when she's sick. I don't say anything because I don't want anyone to know. But I know. I know that I'm hungry. And that all I can think about is lunch.

—Tina

The need for nutrition

- The child who is hungry may steal food or chew on objects such as pencils.

- If she hides her hunger she may be irritable, tired, unable to pay attention.

- If she has given up hope on ever having enough to eat, she may grow angry and resentful because a critical survival need is not being met.

There is no remedy for a child's hunger other than to provide food.

Somewhere, somehow, the child must be fed.

Could the school district start a breakfast program if many students arrive hungry? Could whole grain crackers, cereal, fruit, or peanut butter sandwiches be made available before school, possibly in another room to avoid embarrassing children who need to eat; or could students work in the kitchen in the morning?

Mom and Dad fight a lot. Sometimes they hit each other. That's what I wake up to most days. I get in fights on the bus. The kids pick on me and I have to fight back. That's what my life is like before I come to class. Some days it's worse. You tell me to talk to you about things. Well, every morning is a story—a story I have to tell someone before I can try to get on with my day.

—Elena

The need for communication

- The child who needs to tell her story, may annoy you by not being quiet.

- If she doesn't talk about her troubles, she will worry about them and be distracted.

- If she believes no one cares about her problems, she may be troublesome, constantly acting out.

Children with home problems come to school emotionally loaded. The earlier you deal with it the better.

What short morning class routine could free you to speak with the child, if only for a short time?

Could the student write in a journal on difficult days? You could respond in writing later.

Could you provide peer counselors or arrange time with a close friend?

I live with my grandparents. There are no other children to play with. Weekends are so boring. School is the only chance I get to be with other kids. I'm not very good at making friends—I haven't done it much; but it is exciting to be with everyone. I want to learn to play and talk to other kids. These are the kids I'm going to spend the rest of my life with. I wonder if they'll like me?

—Kyle

The need for socialization

- The child who has an unmet need for socialization may talk constantly.

- If he hides his longing for friends, he may be isolated, a loner.

- If he is frustrated by his inability to make friends, he may be aggressive and set out to make enemies.

Ultimately the child's personal and job success as an adult will be determined more by an ability to get along with others, than by specific skills.

Which children have few opportunities to be with other children outside of school?

Which first-hour activities could be done in pairs or small groups—even if only for selected students?

Which kids have the most to learn from each other, and how can you facilitate this connection?

I have always enjoyed being touched. Mom and Dad used to touch me more, but now they are busy and they say, "You're not a baby anymore." But I like to touch and be touched. I'm rough and physical when I play. My teacher tells me I'm always poking and grabbing kids. But I like to touch. I don't have any brothers to wrestle with at home. I just wish that someone would play with me the way Dad used to when he had time.

—Joey

The need for touch

- The child who longs to be touched, may be constantly touching other children and adults.

- If he hides his need for closeness, he may poke and jab to provoke a physical response.

- If he is angry because he can't get people to touch and hug him, he may be distant and fear being touched.

Touch is the clearest and most direct communication between two people. Perhaps that's why we are never too young or too old to enjoy it and why words will never replace it.

Can you teach your children to give hand and shoulder massages? They could practice on you during story time.

Sit in a circle and teach good touch. Practice giving hugs, walking arm in arm, sitting back-to-back on the floor, shaking hands.

What class activities could begin with a silent group huggle? How about pets in the room?

Dad doesn't laugh much since Mom left last year. He comes home from work with a lot on his mind. He gets upset when I giggle, so I try not to get silly anymore. Friends don't come over these days. Our home is not much fun anymore. So when I go to school I sometimes try to make people laugh. I go to school earlier and earlier these days. Does life really have to be this serious all the time?

—Roderigo

The need for humor

- The child who needs laughter in his life, may become the class clown.

- If he hides his need for humor and fun, he may become overly serious, the "adult" child.

- If he believes he will never find joy and laughter in life, he may appear cynical, morose, or even sadistic.

Humor heals.

There is healing power in laughter. Could you laugh at yourself more often, more heartily? Could you model the human comedy of errors and self-forgiveness?

Are there situations that could be lightened with a joke or a story? How will you do it?

My brother and I live in the city in a small apartment. He's in third grade and likes school. He wakes up at 5:30 each morning, runs around the house and drives us all crazy. I get up at the last moment and drag myself to school. My mind tries to work but my body wants to be in bed. His body wants to work. We're very different, but we're both in trouble with teachers before 9:00.

—Jared

The need for physical activity

- The child who needs physical activity may appear sleepy or overactive.

- If he avoids activity, he may appear listless, unenthusiastic.

- If the need for activity is frustrated, he may appear resistant and unwilling to undertake activities.

All vertebrates stretch to begin the day. Tension flows out of active muscles. All bodies need activity and oxygen to stay awake, and, with kids, all you need to do is provide the occasion.

Could you begin the day with a stretching routine? And repeat it throughout the day?

Could you begin some activities with a series of deep breaths?

You move about the room as you supervise students. Students also need to move frequently. Could you accommodate that need by scheduling short breaks?

My world changes every day. I never know who will be at my house in the morning. Sometimes Mom wakes me up; other times I have to get up by myself. I never know if there will be food for breakfast. Sometimes my sister shares my room; some nights I live with my Dad. I never really know what I will come home to at night, or where we might be next month.

—Juanita

The need for structure

■ The child who is trying to create structure in her life may constantly ask, "What do we do next?"

■ If her need for consistency is hidden, she may be resistant to any change in routine.

■ If she has given up on trying to discover order in her life, she may be chronically unprepared and appear to thrive on chaos.

For many children, school is the one constant in their life, the one structure they can depend upon. You may notice that even those who hate school and everything about it are seldom absent.

Post and review the schedule every day, noting even insignificant changes.

Which children need to be informed individually of any changes in the structure of the day?

Which routines should be followed consistently, every day?

My family argues. Each morning my older sisters fight over the bathroom. Mom doesn't like mornings so she yells at all of us. Dad yells at Mom. The radio in the kitchen drowns out the television in the next room. I walk to school with my Walkman blaring so I don't hear the traffic and sirens in our neighborhood. I come to school already stressed out.

—Philip

The need for relaxation

- The child who needs to relax, may appear reclusive, withdrawn, or exhausted.

- If he doesn't know how to relax, he may remain agitated, nervous, and "wired."

- If he is under severe stress and is frustrated in his efforts to deal with it, he may appear oppositional and despondent.

Relaxation is a direct route to enhanced learning, creative problem solving, anger management, stress management, and general health. It is what we placed kids in "time-out" to acquire. We know now that relaxation must be taught.

Books and tapes are available to help us teach relaxation skills.

How could you include relaxation instruction in your classroom? Deep breathing before a test? Neck and shoulder stretch during a test? Hand massage after a test? A relaxation tape to bring them back to a peaceful world?

Since first grade I have hated school. I don't read well and I'm not very good at math. I make a lot of mistakes. My parents say I'm lazy—that I never try to do my best. I used to try. Now I just do everything I can to avoid work. I don't want anyone to see how stupid I am, so I never turn in my assignments. I know I would just fail anyway. I don't know why they make dumb people like me go to school anyway.

—Kara

The need for encouragement

- The child who needs encouragement may seek constant reassurance.

- If she is afraid of failure, she may say, "I can't," and avoid trying.

- If she becomes discouraged by failure, she will say, "I won't," and refuse to try.

Find the occasion to answer these questions for each child.

What is it you like about me?

How am I unique?

What do I do well?

How can I affect my world?

The four-foot rule

The most important and powerful interactions in an elementary classroom take place among the children, below the four-foot level.

Corollary one:

> What students learn from each other will have more impact and staying power than anything they are told by adults.

Corollary two:

> Severely abused children, children who have learned to mistrust the advice and attention of adults, can only be reached most effectively through peer support and encouragement.

Corollary three:

> Acceptance by adults cannot substitute for acceptance by peers.

Corollary four:

> To have a heart-to-heart conversation with a child, your head and heart must be on the same level as the child's head and heart, below the four-foot level.

Teaching social skills

Social skills training is not just a curriculum. It is the art of turning misbehaviors into social learning opportunities throughout the day.

While more and better social skills curricula are written every year, all the material you need to work with a troubled child can be found in the day's events.

To improve social skills, a troubled child requires direct, corrective feedback on his daily actions.

At recess I don't fit in. I bounce into four or five groups, but I don't know how to make friends so I move on. Or else I stay alone. Sometimes I get frustrated and push someone and then I'm taken inside. That's fine with me. Until someone teaches me how to play, I don't want to be out there anyway. How did you learn to play?

—Kerry

When I see a junior high student who lacks social skills, I can't help wondering what we taught him for eight years that was more important than how to make friends.

The elementary years are optimal for learning social skills: everyone together with one teacher, eager to learn and forgive. With each successive year learning these skills becomes more difficult. By junior high we must gather troubled students in support groups and discuss contrived situations. What are the primary years if not a social skills laboratory?

Identify the behaviors that isolate a child and address them one by one.

Assume that the child does not know the right way. And assume that the child is willing to change.

Assume lack of awareness.

Assume the willingness to change.

Children often lack the concepts to describe the annoying habits of the socially backward child.

"Nathan is just a jerk."
"What does he do that makes him a jerk?"
"He stands too close all the time."
"He violates your space."
"Yeah, he's a jerk. He violates my space."
"Let's teach him not to violate your space."

Teaching the *word* clarifies the *concept*.

Then the problem can be addressed.

Kids who offend other's personal boundaries can be taught to respect others' personal space. Assume lack of awareness.

"Nathan, some kids don't like it when you stand this close to them. Let's practice standing further apart. Good. Now, let's have your friends help you practice."

Assume the willingness to change.

I often enlist a student "consultant" to help me with the socially deprived student. Together the three of us discuss how to learn the ways of the class.

This is delicate. I want the consultant to feel that he is helping me to understand the class better, without making him feel responsible for helping the socially deprived student learn to fit in.

As an example, I might say, "Sean, maybe you can help me. John is new and having a hard time fitting in on the playground. What games does he need to learn to play?" Although Sean is only asked to give advice, he is presented with an opportunity to help further.

The best information about a child often comes directly from other students:

> "Jessie. How come you never play with Kyle?"
> "He doesn't shower. He smells bad."
> "Jessie, let's have a talk. Then we'll talk to Kyle in a minute."

Contract with a child to change personal habits that interfere with social acceptance: not brushing teeth and other hygiene issues, annoying mannerisms, personal appearance. We all rely on friends to help us notice these things.

A troubled child must be led through a step-by-step learning sequence to help him identify and express the emotions he is feeling.

First, identify the emotion without asking for a response: "You look angry."

Next, label a past emotion: Say, "You were angry yesterday when you put your head down on the table," to further clarify the emotion by referring to the child's past experiences. Continue with questions that supply optional words, "Are you angry or sad now?"

Finally ask a question that will help him identify emotional moments: "What are you feeling at this time?" Learning this progression could take months, or even years for some children.

One of the best methods of teaching social behavior is to pick out a positive incident and bring it to the attention of the whole class. "At recess I saw Jason invite Marie to play with the group after he noticed her standing alone." With many troubled kids, this indirect method is less threatening and more powerful than speaking directly to the child.

Reward the socially isolated student with ten minutes of free play time at the end of class, and allow her to invite one or two other students to join her. Watch her circle of friends grow. Call yourself the Social Director of the third grade. And think of this task as an art.

You can teach social skills more effectively in first grade than in third, more successfully in third grade than in sixth. With each year there is more habit, more history to overcome.

Never underestimate the desire of children to help a troubled child once they conceptualize what that child needs to learn and exactly how they can help.

I've stolen from kids all year, but I never got caught. I was good at it. I even got angry whenever you accused me of stealing. But when you asked me if I wanted to do something about my reputation for stealing, what else could I say but "yes." You told the class that I wanted their help to overcome "my bad reputation," and suddenly we could all talk about my "reputation problem" instead of everyone whispering behind my back that I was a thief.

So I agreed to accept consequences for anything stolen in class for four weeks. (That's the result of a bad reputation—getting blamed regardless.) Different classmates were assigned to be with me at all times so I could avoid suspicion, and I agreed to make daily progress reports about our "class project."

After I asked for their help and the class became involved in helping me, I found myself with friends for the first time in my life. Since I would get blamed anyway, and was with classmates who wanted to trust me, I stopped stealing. You see, months ago my only friend was my secret habit.

—Sofia

Four goals of misbehavior

Dreikur's *Four Goals of Misbehavior* is a valuable tool for understanding a student's misbehavior. The beauty of this perspective is that you can identify the goal of the child's misbehavior by looking at your own reaction.

If the child's behavior:

- **annoys you,** the goal is attention. Ignore it.

- **angers you,** the goal is power. Rely upon rules and consequences to remove yourself from the struggle.

- **hurts you,** the goal is revenge. State your feelings and discuss mutual concerns.

- **makes you despair,** the goal is to display inadequacy. Find a way to encourage and empower the child.

Your assessment is correct if your response reduces the misbehavior.

- If you ignore the student and he continues to misbehave, perhaps his goal was not attention but power.

- If cracking down with consequences has no effect, he may be out for revenge.

- If a heart-to-heart discussion fails to move him, his goal may be a display of inadequacy.

- If encouragement doesn't brighten the child, the goal was not to elicit your support. Check out Power or Revenge.

There is far more to the entire concept, but this is the essence. Simple and straightforward, the *Four Goals of Misbehavior* are well worth the few minutes required to memorize them.

Understanding the child's goal, however, is not enough. You must also be able to address the unmet need that prompted the goal.

Peer parenting

Social skills training with troubled children often includes teaching kids and their friends to parent themselves in the absence of effective parenting.

You may encourage peer parenting in a variety of ways: establish phone networks so kids can wake each other, pair students as study buddies, teach parenting skills to children who must care for younger siblings.

Teaching even young children to compensate for poor parenting is often the most direct and effective route to meeting their needs.

After waiting for months, we gave up believing that Angel's mother would ever wake her on time. Although Angel was only a second grader, we bought her an alarm clock and rewarded her at school for arriving on time.

Angel knows she is on her own; so do we.

That's where her education needs to begin.

The most effective way to enhance a parent's skills is through regular reports sent home with the child. These notes coordinate school and home goals, reduce negative behaviors, and subtly introduce new parenting skills. All benefit from them, but most of all the student.

An effective note to the parent will state specifically what happened and how you responded. It will state that no further consequence is necessary. This is especially important if you suspect that the parent punishes severely. The note will ask only that the parents discuss the incident with the child. Close the note with a positive expression of concern and interest in the child.

Dear Mr. and Mrs. Conrad:
Christine has had difficulty at recess this week. She refused to take turns on the swing and argued with the playground supervisor. I spoke with her, and later all the students discussed playground rules and expectations during today's class meeting. She understands that she will lose 5 minutes of time on the swing tomorrow.

No further discipline is needed, but I would appreciate it if you would discuss the importance of sharing playground equipment. She values your opinions and interest.

I have enjoyed the progress your daughter is making this year, and I look forward to seeing her tomorrow.

Troubled children need more than "parent-friends" or "parent-housemates." They need to be children, and they will force their parents to be real parents.

Child abuse can never be condoned, but sometimes it can be understood. Imagine yourself as a young parent with a child who recoils from physical touch, never wants to be held, screams, and cannot be comforted. Think of the maturity it would require to recognize this as the child's disposition and not your failure as a parent. Now imagine being in the house all day with this child for five years. . . .

The abusive parent lacks skills, support, and direction; and needs healing as badly as the child. Condemnation heals no one.

Approximately 80% of all high school students will become parents. Many will primarily influence their community not through their careers, but through their children. In spite of this fact, we fail to give priority to teaching parenting skills; and wonder why they aren't learned instinctively.

Rules and expectations

Class rules are important first statements to the class about expectations for behavior.

Class rules, posted on the wall, set guidelines for the classroom.

Rules are best when they are:

Stated in positive terms. Negative rules (Don't talk; don't chew gum) set an adversarial tone in the room, and serve as a constant reminder of the fastest way to obtain negative attention.

Few in number. No one really likes rules anyway.

Global rather than specific. The rules should be phrased in ways that encompass all positive and all negative behavioral possibilities. If a rule is too specific, children will search for and find alternatives that aren't listed.

Frequently brought to students' attention. The list of rules is the operating manual for the class.

Always try.

Cooperate with others.

During independent work, stay on task and in your seat.

Examples of classroom rules*

*Acknowledgment to R. Sprick for this list of rules.

Class rules are broad guidelines and are only as effective as the student's ability to understand exactly what they mean in practical terms.

As I teach behavioral expectations, I sometimes imagine I am the director of a Broadway play. When a valued actor makes a mistake, I don't fire him and I don't ask him why he made the error. I simply direct him back to the script.

A teacher is the director of the class play. Convey expectations as clearly as possible and as frequently as necessary; point out unacceptable behavior; restate what is expected.

As director, state your expectations in clear businesslike terms. Never scold or sarcastically criticize these sensitive actors: "Remember, third graders always walk carefully with scissors."

After all, you are the third-grade teacher, the authority on this new role that your students are stepping into.

Troubled children require more clear and more frequent direction in their roles than other children.

When a troubled child misbehaves he often is simply ad-libbing a role he never really understood very well from the start. That may sound naive, until you remember how complex and confused the rest of a child's life can be.

The most important task in the first hour of each day, the first day after any vacation, and the first week of the school year is to reaffirm and clarify the class rules and expectations.

Consequences

Incident: The child is out of her seat, overactive, not attentive.

Natural consequence
Do not repeat the information she missed.

Logical consequence
Move her to the front of the room during instruction.

Need-meeting consequence
Allow her to run two laps around gym to work off excess energy.

"Tragic" consequence
Remove her from physical education and recess until she learns to settle down in class.

Incident: Two children repeatedly argue in the hallway.

Natural consequence
Allow the children to settle differences on their own.

Logical consequences
Require that each child write a three-step problem solving model of how to settle their problem.

Need-meeting consequence
Discuss the problem in a class meeting and ask the classmates for suggestions about how to solve the problem.

"Tragic" consequence
Place both students in detention; force them to shake hands; tell them not to do it again.

Behavior contracting

For some teachers behavior contracting is an effective technique for classroom management; for others it is just an unpleasant memory of many long hours spent in tedious behavior modification classes learning convoluted terms and logic.

Contracting, however, is simply one of many tools for behavior management. No single technique is a final solution, but each can be part of the answer.

Behavior contracting can be a highly creative, individual, and caring intervention that can cut to the core of a child's needs. Its only limitations are its history of highly conventional use and your own imagination.

Would you consider a behavior contract if: it took only five minutes each day; it didn't have to involve the whole class; it could extend for only a short period of time; highly creative rewards could be involved; you never had to ad-lib consequences; you could use it to focus on obscure and hard to remove personal behaviors; you knew that the purpose of behavior contracting was not to just control behavior, but to teach the skills of self-intervention?

The following pages describe three different types of behavior contracts for you to consider.

There are three types of behavior contracts: verbal, charted, and written. Each takes no more than a few minutes to design and implement.

Verbal behavior contracts

Verbal contracts inform children of how you will assist them to learn the skills of self-intervention. You might say, for example:

"Students, take 20 minutes for silent study. Joshua, as we've discussed, during independent reading time you know you need to turn your desk to the wall and put away everything that might distract you. I'll check with you in one minute."

Joshua is learning to recognize what he requires to focus his attention. He will use and value this technique throughout his life. You are teaching him self-intervention techniques that will help him to become successful.

You might follow up on other verbal contracts in one of the following ways:

"Jennie, you're starting to clench your fists, raise your voice, and jerk your shoulders. As you know, that is your body telling you that you need to relax before you become more agitated and lose control. We've seen this before, haven't we? Go to the quiet area in the back of the class, sit down in the way we practiced, and breathe slowly and deeply. In a couple of minutes, I will come back and listen to what you are concerned about. Please do that now, Jennie. Thank you."

"Nathan, we talked about how close you stand to other people when you talk to them, haven't we? And we practiced standing farther back so people would be more comfortable with you. During class today, whenever I notice you standing too close, I will call your name and touch my finger to my cheek. That will be our signal and nothing more will be said. You're doing very well and soon you won't need any signal at all. You're looking forward to that, I know."

Charted behavior contracts   Charted contracts will help students learn to manage specific behaviors one at a time.

List the behaviors that cause problems or that isolate the child. You will likely find there are fewer than you thought. That is the first positive benefit of establishing a contract. Then decide which behavior to focus upon first.

Select behaviors to chart. Identify three behavior goals that will remain on the list for an extended time. They might include some of the items that follow: stay in seat, finish work, keep hands to self. Announce the fourth behavior goal each week according to the current need. The fourth item on the list is the real target behavior.

Determine monitor intervals. How often does the behavior occur? Relate the monitor interval to the behavior frequency. What is a reasonable expectation for change?

If the behavior occurs three times per day, monitor by half-day intervals. If it happens three times per hour, monitor hourly. If three times per minute, monitor each minute!—but do this for only a five-minute period two or three times each day.

Design rewards. Design rewards that meet the child's inner needs: time with classmates for withdrawn child; time with you for discouraged child.

The reward must be something the child actually values. Ask the child for suggestions. Insure that rewards are frequent, worthwhile, and consistent.

Implement. Ensure that the child will receive the reward early enough to make him feel successful and to maintain his interest.

Do not give points for successful performance and then take them away as a consequence for later misbehavior. Rewarding an action is like a mini-contract: it is unfair to void it in the future. Removing points is particularly devastating to troubled children.

The power of behavior charting lies in the regularity with which you attend to a child when a specific behavior is being performed correctly. The child realizes that he can improve his world if he focuses his attention on the positive behavior. He then starts to believe that his problems are no longer overwhelming. They can be managed one by one.

Written behavior contracts

Written contracts can be used to correct complex behavior problems. Unlike verbal contracts, written contracts utilize rewards and consequences, and can address behaviors that are more complex than behavior charting can handle.

Set aside all that you labored to learn in your behavior modification class at college. It is not as difficult as it may have sounded. Behavior contracting is simply a business-like way to trade favors. You trade rewards for behaviors the child doesn't need any longer. It's that simple.

You must answer three questions to write a good contract:

- What does the child do that is undesirable and how often does he do it?

- What would you like him to do instead?

- What can you offer him to make the change worthwhile?

Written contracts, like all behavior contracts, must be agreements of mutual benefit. However, unlike verbal contracts, a written contract usually addresses a behavior that is of more concern to the teacher. The student may not believe that this behavior is a problem but will agree to the contract because either the reward is of value or the consequence is undesirable.

When misbehavior has backed a child into a corner, a contract is a face-saving way for the child to move forward; the reward can be the mitigation of an earlier consequence.

Other children seldom mind a troubled student receiving special attention or rewards. They know who is different; they know who is having a hard time. It's no surprise to them. Adults are the ones who think all children should be treated identically. That belief is an adult myth.

I focus my first behavior contract with a student not on the behavior that is really most important but rather on the behavior that bothers me most. When that behavior is removed, I feel better about the student. That serves us both well.

Paul argues with adults often. He is very logical, but he argues small points that divert the discussion. Through logic he controls, avoids, and confuses. We have learned to give him consequences for arguing, regardless of whether the minor point he has seized is right or wrong. His point is not the point.

Ultimately, a contract will be successful if the student recognizes that the new behavior meets his inner needs better that the previous misbehavior. That, not the simple completion of the contract, is the goal.

School-wide discipline programs

School-wide discipline programs, almost by definition, will not meet the needs of troubled children. Consider the following perspectives.

Perhaps the fastest way to identify troubled children is to install a school-wide discipline program. Within a matter of weeks, two kids will be scheduled for detention until adulthood and another one will be expelled before graduating from fifth grade. These are your troubled kids.

School-wide discipline deals with misbehavior in a logical, rational, and consistent manner. For misbehavior that is logical, rational, and consistent, it is very effective. However, troubled children don't misbehave logically.

A programmed response to all misbehavior inhibits the creativity necessary to deal with troubled children. In reality, most school-wide discipline programs:

- become overly dependent upon punishment,

- foster the false belief that you now have an effective response to all misbehavior,

- inhibit more creative responses to specific behaviors,

- fail to address underlying needs,

- fail to teach adaptive and corrective skills,

- become impersonal and disempowering for the teachers.

Troubled children tend to make shambles of school-wide discipline programs because of their illogical response to key components.

Loss of privileges: Children who feel they have nothing are not afraid of losing anything, or everything.

Warnings: A troubled child will either perceive a warning as a "freebie," and conclude that if he got away with it once he could probably get away with it again; or have as great an emotional outburst to the warning as he would to the punishment itself.

Ultimatums: The sharper students who understand power recognize the inherent fallacies in many school-wide discipline programs: you simply cannot, for instance, expel a fourth-grader for a succession of minor incidents.

Detention: Again, sharper students realize that 10 days of detention have to be served, but 40 or 80 days will ultimately force the administration to produce an alternative solution.

Emotional detachment: Troubled children will ultimately become resentful of the detachment involved in a "system" that disciplines. They may, indeed, have an unhealthy need for your emotional reactions to them; but they also have a sincere need for caring, adult involvement in their lives. Removing troubled children from school only confirms the children's belief that they are unworthy and that the school is unwilling to search for their inner value.

Consequences: Most school-wide consequences are based on the following assumptions: removal from peers at recess is a punishment, time in detention is unpleasant, expulsion or afternoon detention will inconvenience parents and elicit their support, taking away noon activity or something a child really likes will encourage him to do better.

Each of these assumptions may or may not be true for a troubled child. You cannot assume a logical response with a troubled child.

Expectations: Working with a troubled child is a constant search for any progress beyond previous behavior. For a child who in the past struck teachers when angry, swearing when angry is a significant step forward. You are not obliged to accept swearing, but you'd have to admit that it's an improvement over previous forms of tension release. A programmed response to swearing will not allow you to adjust to such individual circumstances.

Misbehavior is relative to previous behavior. Progress, however slight, must be rewarded.

School-wide contingencies for misbehavior may save you from making rash decisions, but they shouldn't prevent you from formulating creative alternatives.

Remove truly troubled children from the school-wide program before they succeed in making a mockery of it.

Physical restraint

Physical restraint should be reserved exclusively for angry, out-of-control behavior—when the child is a danger to himself or others. In these circumstances, it is indispensable.

Physical restraint is a therapeutic procedure that, for proper use, requires training. This section can only present an introduction to its potential value and is not intended as a substitute for skilled training.

Physical restraint is not a discipline procedure. Restraint is a physical expression of control that should be used only with children who experience uncontrolled anger. When a child is clearly endangering himself or others, an adult must either assume physical control or call for assistance. Assuming physical control of an out-of-control student is an administrative necessity that can have a tremendous therapeutic value when it is administered correctly.

Try to imagine the well of anger within me. No, you can't; you haven't lived my life. Just imagine some- thing bottomless, powerful, and all consuming. Now imagine the terror I live with every day that suddenly, at any moment, I will be thrown again into my lifetime of anger. It takes so little. I strike out. I yell and scream, throw chairs, hit people. My rage is beyond my control. I fear what I'll do—hurt others, myself.

Adults surround me, yet they back away. They fear an anger they have never felt. I am out of control, and adults are powerless to stop me.

You grab me, wrap my arms, and hold me. But I know you'll let me go. My anger is too much for you. You'll push me away, like other adults. I'll make you. I struggle against you, against my anger, against my world. I call you whore, bastard. I hate you. I'll kill you. You hold me. I struggle.

I struggle to break free from you, from my life, from my anger, with all my strength, until I can struggle no more. I cry, spent, exhausted. While you hold me, I am deep in my hurt and vulnerable. I have survived my anger. Slowly I regain control. The hurt? Yes. I feel it and must face it, but no longer the fear. The cycle of fear is broken. It is not all powerful, and I am not alone.

—Bart

Physical restraint procedure

Here's how to use physical restraint safely and effectively:

- Face the child. With your right hand, reach across to his right hand. Pull while spinning him so his back is to you.

- Wrap both the child's arms in front of him so that he hugs himself. Rapidly, switch your grip to the child's opposite hand. Grasp him firmly at the base of each hand, just below the wrist, so his hand will not slip out of your circular grip.

- Bend to one knee and place your other one behind the child's closest knee to assist him down. Then seat him on the floor between your legs or you may sit on a low chair with the child on the floor in front of you. Protect his back from hitting your chair.

- Hold the child tightly to your chest with your face safely held away. *Be extremely careful not to put forward strain to the child's neck.*

- If he rocks or kicks, wrap your legs around him to spread-eagle his legs and immobilize his lower body.

- Do not respond to his comments; do not talk about what happened. Say only this: "When you can control yourself, I'll let you go."

Duration: Restrain a child only if you are willing to stay with him until he is in control and completely relaxed. The first time it may take up to an hour or two for him to exhaust himself and regain control.

By the third or fourth time it may take only a matter of minutes. By then he knows if he loses control you will hold him until he regains it.

Preparation: Secure training from local medical personnel. Inform parents of your intention to use restraint and explain the procedure. Demonstrate the use of restraint to all building personnel so they are aware of your intentions. Designate a student to inform both the office and the teacher who will cover your class. Have the student give a prearranged signal to the teacher to avoid lengthy explanations.

Prepare for and practice this procedure, because your single responsibility while restraining must be to the child you are holding.

Often full restraint is not necessary. Once familiar with the procedure, a child may regain control when his arms are immobilized at his sides or held firmly on his desk. If the child kicks, however, protect yourself by placing the child on the ground.

Apply restraint where the problem occurs. If you attempt to move the child anywhere else you greatly increase the possibility of harm to him or to yourself.

Ignore screams of anger. Do not respond. Other students may be concerned, but they will see that you are calm and in control. Remember: the child's anger is not news to them! Most importantly, they will see the child return to class after he has regained control.

Occasionally a child will seem to seek out physical restraint. If you suspect this, increase the amount of positive touch you provide during the day. And keep in mind that even if he continues occasionally to express his anger in your arms, this is a far more therapeutic release than punching walls or other children.

What the child experiences: The child, who was restrained by a caring adult, has been safely guided through a traumatic experience. He has experienced a profound release of anger; has become aware of his inner hurt; and has recovered self control.

He has learned that someone cares enough to hold him while he is in a crisis.

What you experience: You experience the child's anger, calmly. Though it may be physically strenuous, it is a richly rewarding and intimately bonding experience.

Your relationship with this child will never be the same as before; you have held him through his anger.

Author's note: School and state guidelines vary on the use of physical restraint in the classroom. The reader is responsible for knowing the local laws. This book is not meant to supersede any established policy.

Reframing

a paradoxical intervention

All misbehaviors have or can be imagined to have some positive function. Through positive connotation and reframing you allow optimistic descriptions of misbehavior to guide your response.

Through an alternative description of a negative behavior, reframing helps you and the child to view an event more constructively. It is the art of wishful thinking, a play of thoughts and words that can turn a discouraging event into a dynamic new beginning.

Reframing asks others to believe the barely plausible:

> "I think you knew that wall needed color, and that's why you put graffiti on it."

You draw from your intuitive insight (or imagination!) to create a suspension of belief in the mind of the child:

> "I think you tease Karla so she doesn't feel left out and alone."

You make a saint of a sinner:

> "You are too sensitive to have hit Karla any more than what you did."

All the while recognize that what you say may seem ridiculous to others:

> "John hits kids as his way of showing affection."

Learning to reframe misbehavior is only half the fun. The real fun is in the eyes of the child!

Reframing gives opportunities to compliment the hard-to-compliment children, opportunities for them to see themselves in a positive light.

Reframing must not be sarcastic. You must believe in what you say. Sarcastically saying, "You really made her day with that impromptu haircut, Carl," may seem humorous, but not to a sensitive child.

Sarcasm has no place in your work with troubled kids.

A low-point in my career occurred when I confronted Eric, a six foot, violent 16-year-old, in the closed quarters of the psychiatric ward's nurses station. Files everywhere, no room for restraint, and no chance of assistance—I was on my own. Eric turned to me, eyes glazed, hovering on the edge of sanity, and said, "I'm going to tear this room apart, and I'm going to begin with you." He meant it; I knew it. It didn't look good.

So I laughed and said, "You sure could, no doubt about it, but you haven't yet and that tells me you're still in control. You are in control and you have stopped yourself." And reframing saved, at the very least, my day.

Humor and reframing: indispensable when working with troubled kids.

All through first grade, I tried to get out of going to school. I faked sickness and refused to leave home in the morning. Everyone thought I was a liar. When the counselor told me I did it to keep my mom company, I knew someone finally understood. She and Dad fight all the time, and I'm afraid she'll get hurt if I'm not there. The counselor decided to let me call home anytime of the day and see if she was all right. I didn't need to misbehave, I needed to protect my mom.

—Jeff

The positive reframing of a child's behavior may help clarify what the child has long considered to be his true intentions.

Prescribing the symptom

a paradoxical intervention

Prescribing the symptom, is a form of paradoxical intervention in which you permit or request that an undesirable behavior continue. If you can't remove a misbehavior, condone it. If you can't control its disappearance, control its appearance.

Prescribe the symptom only after numerous other attempts to eliminate the behavior have failed.

Simon slept during class. Everything we did to stop him from sleeping failed. Finally we decided to let him sleep. He slept through P.E. and lunch. When he asked why we didn't wake him, we told him we thought he must have needed the sleep. Soon sleeping through class lost all its power, all its appeal, and he chose to stay awake.

But prescribing the symptom is a bold move and must be thought out carefully.

To quiet the class clown I required that he step in front of the class and entertain us for two minutes. He loved it; I felt rather foolish. So next time I told him to do it for ten minutes. He became very uncomfortable by the end. That's the way it should work, I thought. But I was uneasy with embarrassing him that way. He had a need to try to make the class laugh, so each week now I schedule a three-minute comedy time in which he tells us jokes. We all look forward to it.

A good intervention, whether simple or sophisticated, must have heart. It must come from a place of caring. If it fails to honor the student or fails to honor you, apologize and let it go.

Paradoxical interventions help you become an ally of the students, not the victim of their behavior. You become confederates. It is your job to point out the hidden positive that you both know exists in the negative behavior.

John is another irrepressible class clown. I meet with him weekly to discuss his future career as a comedian. We discuss timing, when his jokes work, and when they get him in trouble. We critique subject matter: "Snot jokes used to work in third grade, but the response is inconsistent in fifth grade, isn't it John?" He's in training and I'm his coach. We're a team.

Class meetings

Class meetings allow you to enhance students' communication skills. You make yourself the facilitator of growth rather than the administrator of order—a fresh breath of air for everyone.

In my ideal school, I would start class meetings in the kindergarten and continue them throughout all grades.

In class meetings the teachers would help kids learn to discuss and resolve their own problems. Each teacher would reap the benefits of the previous year. A twenty-minute class meeting each week would make a major impact on a school.

The procedure is simple: post a blank agenda on the wall. When problems among students or other class issues arise, a student writes it on the agenda. It's that simple.

Class meetings help children learn the skills to communicate effectively with each other, and certainly this is a major goal of teaching. They are particularly useful with children who are resistant, for whatever reason, to learning social skills from adults. Students can add a problem to the agenda, know that it will be addressed, and therefore be able to set it aside for a day or two.

Often, setting the issue aside brings resolution without your facilitation. Students learn that many emergencies are resolved with time.

In chairs or on the floor, a circular seating arrangement works best. Change the setting to evoke a change in communication style and personal expectations.

In class meetings we bring out concerns, feelings, problem solving, and, yes, laughter. We speak of our futures together.

Swearing can be dealt with at the class meeting. Most kids swear for the effect it has on classmates. When other kids tell them they don't like to hear them swear, it loses all its power. Young children will often stop immediately.

If you want ideas about rewards or consequences for troubled behaviors, ask the class for suggestions. They have their own perception of the importance of certain issues; you are guaranteed a highly creative response. In fact whenever you feel at a loss, ask the kids for direction.

If you're tired of snuffing out student conflict in order to maintain order, becoming the class meeting facilitator may be just the role you seek. It may change your view of the teaching profession.

And, no, you don't need to be a trained counselor—just a perceptive observer and a good listener. You must be willing to risk; you must be willing to share.

Videotaping helps children to be aware of their actions and encourages them to practice new behaviors. Videotape your class meetings (with permission). You'll be amazed at what you'll notice when watching the tape later. Videotaping is the best available tool to move children beyond their denial of classroom misbehavior, and to remove yourself from confrontation over past events.

Stinkin' Thinkin'

Stinkin' Thinkin' is a term you can use with children to conceptualize negative thinking and negative self-talk.

We do a good job at eliminating most swearing in classrooms but are less successful with other words that can be far more destructive:

"I can't."
"I'm no good at math."
"I'm a jerk."
"Nobody likes me."
"I never win."
"Shut up stupid."
"I hate everybody."

These words program the mind with negative expectations. As we teach children to be responsible for misbehavior, we can also teach them to take responsibility for how they mis-talk and program their own failure.

After they learn to identify negative thinking and irrational beliefs, children can be taught to recognize defeatist phrases and turn them into positive statements.

Avoid generalities: don't say "We never win," say "We lost today."

Avoid negative predictions: don't say "We'll never win," say "I hope we start winning soon."

Specify concerns: don't say "Nobody likes me," say "I'd like to make more friends."

Positive self-statements: don't say "I always make mistakes," say "I'm still learning."

Teach positive affirmations and self-talk as a companion to identifying Stinkin' Thinkin'. Explore cognitive behavioral materials for ideas.

Since the perpetrator and the victim are the same person, abusive self-talk is one form of child abuse we can effectively deal with in the schools.

Time in

Removing a child from positive reinforcement for misbehavior (time-out) can lead to other forms of self-intervention

Time out: so useful, so misused.

We throw angry children into time-out and expect them to come back relaxed. But relaxation is a skill; working through anger is a skill. How do we expect them to learn these things?

Rather than misusing time-out by extending it beyond three to five minutes, why not incorporate relaxation training and problem solving into it and call it "time-in." Then time-out can remain the brief interruption of reinforcement; time-in can be a direction to self-intervene on a cognitive level.

Call the time-out area a relaxation area and teach kids the skills you want them to learn. Allow them to choose time-in when they recognize the need to self-intervene. Give each student two time-in tokens good for two minutes anytime during the day.

Teach progressive muscle relaxation, visualization, autogenic instruction—"I'm telling my hands to relax"—and deep breathing. These are the same techniques they'll use as adults to manage pain or to control high blood pressure. If we teach these techniques now, they won't have to learn them later.

Rites of passage

A child's perception of personal growth is accompanied by heightened self-expectations. We can actively create the expectation of impending change.

Our culture lacks rites of passage, acknowledgments of growth and maturation. I often construct rites of passage when expectations will change for children.

Rites of passage can be constructed in many ways: change the seating arrangement during the year to suggest an increase in trust and responsibility, change discipline procedures for the older grades in the school, address students differently in the second half of the year by using Mr. and Ms., for instance, or by avoiding nicknames.

With a rite of passage give form and occasion to the personal change that you hope to see.

All students consider themselves to have been years younger just months earlier. Point out to them how much they have changed and you can put them years ahead:

> "Third grade will be a big change for you. Remember last fall when you used to yell and scream when you were a second grader? It will be different for you next year."

> "You're getting too old to . . ."

> "Isn't it time you let that go?"

> "When do you think you'll stop . . ."

I use such statements often and I have always found students' responses to be fruitful.

Empowerment

affecting
the world

Growth and change occur only when the child is empowered with the belief that they can occur.

Powerful children want to learn the small and large ways that they can affect their world.

Powerful children draw strength from knowing people who take risks, who have created the lives they would want to live.

Children are empowered through reminders of their powerful moments—memories of past accomplishments and adventures, objects such as gifts and awards, or special clothing that reminds them of who they are and what they want to become.

Children are empowered when given daily opportunities to demonstrate who they have become, what they have already created in their lives, and what they want their lives to be.

Powerful children enjoy opportunities to help others.

Powerful children know the value of a strong body and healthy daily routines.

Powerful children like to talk about their concerns about the future, and look for reassurance that the world will be there for them when they grow into it.

These are experiences powerful children know; they are the experiences troubled children seek.

Let me show you what I've created in my life already, and what I want my life to be.

Catch the humor

You must catch the humor when:

you threaten to expel a fifth-grade boy who would like nothing better;

a boy in centerfield stops long enough to stick out his tongue just for you;

you suspend a child after four hours of misbehavior;

it is you who needs the afternoon off;

five well-paid professionals gather at a table to discuss a fifth-grader's disturbing flatulence;

you know that your fourth-grade gang of boys will someday sit on the porch of an old-folks home and discuss the tricks they pulled on you.

You must catch the humor in:

reminding a child to put his name at the top of his paper and being called an SOB.

You must catch the humor that they miss.

There is no greater challenge than teaching a troubled child. If you're willing to be creative, to risk, to try and fail and try again, working with a troubled child can teach you more, and touch you more deeply than any other encounter.

Companion resources from Whole Person Associates

62 Ways to Create Change in the Lives of Troubled Children
L. Tobin, MEd

Focus on the child, not the behavior

Find quick responses to misbehavior with this "on-the-spot" desktop reference. A powerful companion piece to *What Do You Do with a Child Like This?*, this flip book features practical guidelines for teachers, counselors, and parents. Each page includes creative approaches for handling misbehavior and an affirming quote to help build the child's self-esteem.
62W / $12.95

Wellness Activities for Youth, Volumes 1 and 2
Sandy Queen

Teach young people how to make healthy lifestyle choices

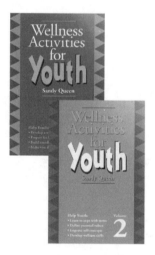

Curriculum developer Sandy Queen designed these whole-person, "no-put-down" activities to help young people make healthy choices about physical and emotional health, relationships, stress management, substance abuse, and more. Ideal for kids from upper elementary to senior high, and many exercises can be adapted for families, as well.
WY1N / $29.95 (volume 1)
WY1W / $12.95 (worksheet masters)

WY2N / $29.95 (volume 2)
WY2W / $12.95 (worksheet masters)

Call 1-800-247-6789 for a complete catalog.

Whole Person Associates ■ 210 West Michigan ■ Duluth, MN 55802-1908
800-247-6789 ■ 218-727-0500 ■ 218-727-0505 FAX
E-mail: books@wholeperson.com ■ Web site: http://www.wholeperson.com